UP and DOWN, ROUND and ROUND:

A book about understanding + identifying emotions

SARA OLSHER

All day, every day, our emotions go **up** and **down.**

HAPPY!

let's get breakfast!

wake up time...

sleepy

Wake up, Stuart...

I don't want to get dressed!

GRUMPY

We feel emotions in our bodies, and then our brains decide what they mean.

Our bodies send us signals to help us notice our feelings.

I don't want to go to school. my legs feel like jelly.

WORRIED

my tummy hurts. I hate goodbye.

Sad

When our chest feels tight,
our brain might decide we are nervous, or maybe excited.

Our emotions help us understand the world
and make decisions about what to do.

We all have emotions. They aren't good or bad.
Some emotions have a lot of energy, like anger or excitement.
Your body wants to jump or run or yell or kick!

CREATIVE

bored... sooo bored...

Excited!

IMPATIENT

Other emotions have low energy, like sadness or loneliness.
Those feelings might make us want to lay down or sleep.

HAPPY!

my heart is pounding! I love recess!

Excited!

We can use colors to describe our emotions, and whether they have high energy or low energy.

Maybe we don't know the name of our emotion right away, but we know it makes us feel red or yellow (high energy) or blue (low energy).

Usually, we're in the green, ready to play or learn.

my tummy kind of hurts

NERVOUS

my face is getting hot. my fists are clenched.

ANGRY! IT WAS MY TURN!

Some emotions *feel* better than others. It's normal to want red or blue feelings, like sadness or anger, to go away.

But all of our emotions are important! They help us understand the world and make good decisions about what to do next.

No one feels happy all the time.

SHY

when I think about reading aloud, my tummy feels squishy...

Emotions happen for a lot of reasons.

Sometimes we have emotions because of
what's happening around us.

PROUD

I feel buzzy and tingly all over!

my tummy is soft and warm.

Calm

Sometimes we have emotions because we need something.
Maybe we are hungry and need a snack. Maybe we are tired and
need to rest. Maybe we are lonely and need a hug.

And sometimes, we **create** emotions by thinking thoughts.

We might remember a happy memory
and start to feel warm inside.

Or start to worry about something,
and feel sick in our tummy.

I miss my family. I want to go home! My chest feels heavy. There's a rock in my tummy.

Sad

JOYFUL

Lunch is soon... WAIT! There's a treat at lunch today!

HUNGRY

My tummy is rumbling.

Did you know when we name what we are feeling, we can affect our emotions? Naming emotions makes unpleasant emotions not last as long, and helps us to enjoy the pleasant emotions more.

ANGRY!

my body is tight. my hands are FISTS!

And when we know what we're feeling, we can make different choices about how we act.

Like maybe **not** yelling at our parents or hitting our sister or breaking something when we're angry.

Naming emotions puts you in charge of your emotions, instead of your emotions being in charge of you.

Some scientists think there are over 84,000 emotions! Luckily we don't need to name all of those.

Here are some of the more common emotions (and their colors!).

CONFUSED

CREATIVE

Sad

depressed.

UNCOMFORTABLE

With so many emotions every day,
there's lots of time to practice.

Understanding what we are feeling and where emotions live in our bodies takes practice. Many *grown-ups* still don't know what they're feeling, because they never learned how to stop and feel their emotions.

It's *very important* to pay attention to our feelings, because that's how we let emotions go. When we know how to let them go, they don't control us.

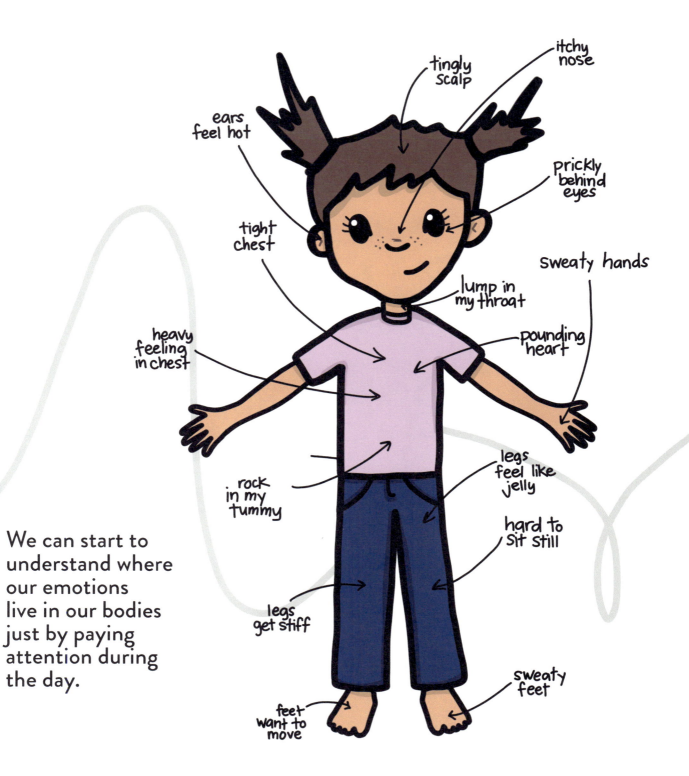

We can start to understand where our emotions live in our bodies just by paying attention during the day.

Sometimes big emotions can scare us. We worry that the emotion in our body will get too big or strong, or it will never end.

But no feeling lasts forever - even the really big ones.

When we have big feelings and big emotions, getting that energy *out* by crying or running or kicking a ball can make us feel better. So can talking about our feelings or getting a hug from a safe person. A grown-up can handle our big feelings.

Everyone's emotions are different, because everyone's body and brain are different — and our bodies and brains make us feel our emotions.

Some people don't often feel strong emotions.
They feel their emotions somewhere in the middle - just
a little bump up or a little bump down.

Some people feel really big feelings.
When they get angry, they get VERY angry.
When they get sad, they get VERY sad.
And when they feel happy, they feel VERY happy.

Some people feel high energy emotions more easily than others. They might feel **anxious** or **worried** more easily.

And some people feel low energy emotions more easily than others. They might feel sad or depressed more easily.

Everyone's body and brain are different.
Which do you think you are most like?

GRUMPY

WORRIED

CREATIVE

PROUD

FOCUSED

And at the end of every day,
we can remember our day was full of all kinds of emotions.

Some felt pleasant, some felt unpleasant, some felt
confusing, and some we didn't notice at all.

No day is all good or all bad and every day is different.

How do **you** feel?

FURIOUS!

Excited!

IMPATIENT

Calm

SHY

UNCOMFORTABLE

depressed.

Sad

Hi! My name is Sara. Nice to meet you!

I wrote this book (& lots of others!) because I like to draw + help people.

Things I LOVE!

- reading
- Dancing (Badly)
- my family
- nature
- animals
- candy
- Rainbows
- Quiet time

I do all my drawings on an iPad with an Apple pencil

I live in a state known for trees + rain, in a city nicknamed "the cherry city."

I live with my daughter and our two cats, Waffle + Batman.

One day, I want a goat, and I want to name him CAULIFLOWER!

Hey Parents!

You don't have to be a superhero to be an *incredible* parent.

There's no shortage of parenting information out there.
But most of us feel like we can barely make it through the day
... let alone thoughtfully develop the skills our kids need.

At Mighty + Bright, we've figured out how to:

- Incorporate emotional + mental wellbeing into your day-to-day life

- Learn a common language with your kids

- Make your parenting life easier

- Reduce meltdowns and underlying anxiety

     ...with no thick parenting books,
     (and no digital parenting courses.)

Find more books like this and tools that'll totally change your family

SCAN THIS USING YOUR PHONE
or visit: mightyandbright.com/emotions

We believe it shouldn't take *more* effort to guide your kids the way you want to guide them.
It just takes a different perspective.

Book Sara for school visits and
public speaking at saraolsher.com

mighty + bright™

Published by Mighty + Bright
mightyandbright.com

ISBN: 979-8-9851984-2-3

want to tell
Sara something?
send a letter!

Sara Olsher
13203 SE 172ND Ave
Suite 166, #1121
Happy Valley, Oregon
97086